# Essential
# Celtic
# Prayers

## THOMAS McPHERSON

PARACLETE PRESS
BREWSTER, MASSACHUSETTS

2017 First Printing
*Essential Celtic Prayers*

Copyright © 2017 by Paraclete Press, Inc.

ISBN 978-1-61261-926-2

Library of Congress Cataloging-in-Publication Data

Names: Paraclete Press.
Title: Essential Celtic prayers.
Description: Brewster MA : Paraclete Press Inc., 2017.
Identifiers: LCCN 2016057963 | ISBN 9781612619262 (trade paper)
Subjects: LCSH: Prayers. | Celts--Religion.
Classification: LCC BV245 .E75 2017 | DDC 242/.80089916--dc23
LC record available at https://lccn.loc.gov/2016057963

10  9  8  7  6  5  4  3  2  1

Published by Paraclete Press
Brewster, Massachusetts
www.paracletepress.com
Printed in the United States of America

# Introduction

People from all faiths and none at all find in the Celtic tradition an expression of spirituality deeply connected to nature and vibrantly alive—a spiritual rootedness we long for in the twenty-first century, at the same time simpler and richer. This book is a collection of some of the most beautiful and beloved prayers of Celtic Christianity, which speak to us across the centuries.

Celtic Christianity emerged in a time and place where nature was ever-present—in the seasonal harvest and disruptions of it, in the sometimes brutal climate, and in all the gifts from the earth. In their simple rural life, the Celtic Christians were surrounded by the cycles of nature: the seasons, lunar months, tides, dawn and dusk. Even in ordinary tasks like gardening, metalworking, sheep herding, and farm chores, they felt God's sacred presence all around in the natural world.

Many of the prayers in this volume have been passed down and adapted through the centuries. A few have been codified in the regular prayer life of Christians today as liturgical prayers and hymns. Some have been preserved thanks to the *Carmina Gadelica*, a volume of prayers, blessings, charms, and other sacred texts collected in the latter half of the nineteenth century by folklorist Alexander Carmichael. These are presented here with the language updated somewhat. All offer us a distinct perspective on the divine, imbued with nature and focused on the Trinity.

# May the Road
# Rise Up to
# Meet You

# The Original

Perhaps the best-known Celtic prayer is the classic blessing "May the Road Rise Up to Meet You." With its hopeful and forward-looking message, it is often used at weddings, sometimes in musical form. There are many versions; the original is this simple six-line version:

> May the road rise up to meet you.
> May the wind be always at your back.
>
> May the sun shine warm upon your face,
> the rain fall soft upon your fields.
>
> And until we meet again,
> may God hold you in the palm of his hand.

# A Popular Version

The most common version known today, which may or may not trace back to the early Celtic church, is quite a bit longer.

May the road rise up to meet you,
May the wind be always at your back.
May the sun shine warm upon your face,
The rains fall soft upon your fields.

And until we meet again,
May God hold you in the palm of his hand.
May God be with you and bless you;
May you see your children's children.

May you be poor in misfortune,
Rich in blessings,
May you know nothing but happiness
From this day forward.

May the road rise to meet you
May the wind be always at your back
May the warm rays of sun fall upon your home
And may the hand of a friend always be near.

May green be the grass you walk on,
May blue be the skies above you,
May pure be the joys that surround you,
May true be the hearts that love you.

# Peace

# Deep peace and Rutter's "A Gaelic Blessing"

When thinking of Celtic prayers in hymn form, there's a good chance someone will land on John Rutter's 1978 "A Gaelic Blessing," with its evocative and quintessentially Celtic words loaded with links between the divine and nature. The last few lines shift the focus to Christ, but Rutter added these. He says the central words are based on a Celtic rune (poem). In fact, Rutter's first lines appear about halfway through a longer prayer in the 1895 novel *The Dominion of Dreams: Under the Dark Star* by William Sharp (writing as Fiona Macleod.)[1]

> Deep peace of the running wave to you.
> Deep peace of the flowing air to you.
> Deep peace of the quiet earth to you.

Whether Rutter and Sharp both drew from an ancient source, or Sharp authored his own and Rutter took from the nineteenth-century prayer, it is part of the Celtic tradition, because Sharp was a key player in the Celtic Revival, a resurgence of interest in Celtic spirituality and all things Gaelic which began in the late nineteenth century and continues to this day.

In *The Dominion of Dreams*, the main character is facing an amadan—a fairy from Irish folklore—and offers this prayer to subdue it.

(Note that in the phrase "Yellow Shepherd," *yellow* means lucky; and *haughty* in "Haughty Father" means lofty or most high, without the negative connotation it carries today.)

Deep peace I breathe into you,
O weariness, here:
O ache, here!
Deep peace, a soft white dove to you;
Deep peace, a quiet rain to you;
Deep peace, an ebbing wave to you!
Deep peace, red wind of the east from you;
Deep peace, grey wind of the west to you;
Deep peace, dark wind of the north from you;
Deep peace, blue wind of the south to you!
Deep peace, pure red of the flame to you;
Deep peace, pure white of the moon to you;
Deep peace, pure green of the grass to you;
Deep peace, pure brown of the earth to you;
Deep peace, pure grey of the dew to you,
Deep peace, pure blue of the sky to you!
Deep peace of the running wave to you,
Deep peace of the flowing air to you,
Deep peace of the quiet earth to you,
Deep peace of the sleeping stones to you!
Deep peace of the Yellow Shepherd to you,
Deep peace of the Wandering Shepherdess to you,
Deep peace of the Flock of Stars to you,

Deep peace from the Son of Peace to you,
Deep peace from the heart of Mary to you,
And from Briget of the Mantle
Deep peace, deep peace!
And with the kindness too of the Haughty Father
Peace!
In the name of the Three who are One,
Peace!
And by the will of the King of the Elements,
Peace! Peace!

# Peace between Neighbors

Peace between neighbors,
Peace between kindred.
Peace between lovers,
In love of the King of life.

Peace between person and person,
Peace between wife and husband,
Peace between woman and children,
The peace of Christ above all peace.

Bless, O Christ, my face,
Let my face bless every thing;
Bless, O Christ, mine eye,
Let mine eye bless all its sees.

# There Will Be Peace

If there is righteousness in the heart,
there will be beauty in the character.
If there is beauty in the character,
there will be harmony in the home.
If there is harmony in the home,
there will be order in the nation.
If there is order in the nation,
there will be peace in the world.
So let it be!

# You Are the Peace

This first-millennium Celtic prayer has been used many times in traditional hymns and contemporary worship.

You are the peace of all things calm
You are the place to hide from harm
You are the light that shines in dark
You are the heart's eternal spark
You are the door that's open wide
You are the guest who waits inside
You are the stranger at the door
You are the calling of the poor
You are my Lord and with me still
You are my love, keep me from ill
You are the light, the truth, the way
You are my Saviour this very day.

# The Rock of Rocks

Air Carraig nan al,
  Sith Pheadail is Phail,
  Sheumais is Eoin na baigh,
  Is na lan ionraic Oigh,
  Na lan ionraic Oigh.

Sith Athar an aigh,
  Sith Chriosda na pais,
  Sith Spiorad nan gras,
  Duinn fein is do 'n al ta og,
  Duinn fein is do 'n al ta og.

On the Rock of rocks,
  The peace of Peter and Paul,
  Of James and John the beloved,
  And of the pure perfect Virgin,
  The pure perfect Virgin.

The peace of the Father of joy,
  The peace of the Christ of passion,
  The peace of the Spirit of grace,
  To ourselves and to our children,
  Ourselves and our children.

# Loricas

*LORICAS*

The Latin word *lorica* means "military armor for the upper body." In the Celtic Christian tradition, a *lorica* is a protection prayer, that is, a prayer you say to ask for God's protection from some enemy—including the Enemy. You say it in order to be armed and protected for battle against the dark forces. These *loricas* often include lines specifically linking physical body armor to protection from spiritual foes.

# St. Patrick's Breastplate

There's a Celtic prayer perhaps as familiar and beloved as "May the Road Rise up to Meet You," but most people don't know its source. At some point, in some context, you've very likely heard these words sung or prayed:

> Christ beside me,
> Christ before me,
> Christ behind me,
>
> Christ within me,
> Christ beneath me,
> Christ above me.

These exact lines or ones inspired by them have been used in numerous worship songs across many traditions. They are beloved for their gentle and universal tone, echoing a thread that runs through so much Celtic spirituality: God is everywhere around us always. This focus on God's immanence is the foundation for Celtic spirituality's reverence for nature as well as the idea that there is that of God within each of us.

The source of these few lines is a *lorica* commonly called St. Patrick's Breastplate. It dates back at least to the eighth century, and tradition assigns its authorship to St. Patrick in the fifth century, giving the prayer its common name.

There are many versions of the full prayer. Here is a common one.

I arise today
Through a mighty strength, the invocation of the Trinity,
Through the belief in the threeness,
Through confession of the oneness
Of the Creator of Creation.

I arise today
Through the strength of Christ's birth with his baptism,
Through the strength of his crucifixion with his burial,
Through the strength of his resurrection with his ascension,
Through the strength of his descent for the judgment of
    Doom.

I arise today
Through the strength of the love of Cherubim,
In obedience of angels,
In the service of archangels,
In hope of resurrection to meet with reward,
In prayers of patriarchs,
In predictions of prophets,
In preaching of apostles,
In faith of confessors,
In innocence of holy virgins,
In deeds of righteous men.

I arise today
Through the strength of heaven:

Light of sun,
Radiance of moon,
Splendor of fire,
Speed of lightning,
Swiftness of wind,
Depth of sea,
Stability of earth,
Firmness of rock.

I arise today
Through God's strength to pilot me:
God's might to uphold me,
God's wisdom to guide me,
God's eye to look before me,
God's ear to hear me,
God's word to speak for me,
God's hand to guard me,
God's way to lie before me,
God's shield to protect me,
God's host to save me
From snares of devils,
From temptations of vices,
From everyone who shall wish me ill,
Afar and anear,
Alone and in multitude.

I summon today all these powers between me and those evils,
    Against every cruel and merciless power that may oppose
        my body and soul,
    Against incantations of false prophets,
    Against black laws of pagandom,
    Against false laws of heretics,
    Against craft of idolatry,
    Against spells of witches and smiths and wizards,
    Against every knowledge that corrupts man's body and
        soul.
    Christ to shield me today
    Against poison, against burning,
    Against drowning, against wounding,
    So that there may come to me abundance of reward.

Christ with me,
    Christ before me,
    Christ behind me,
    Christ in me,
    Christ beneath me,
    Christ above me,
    Christ on my right,
    Christ on my left,
    Christ when I lie down,
    Christ when I sit down,
    Christ when I arise,
    Christ in the heart of every man who thinks of me,

Essential Celtic Prayers

Christ in the mouth of everyone who speaks of me,
Christ in every eye that sees me,
Christ in every ear that hears me.

I arise today
Through a mighty strength, the invocation of the Trinity,
Through belief in the threeness,
Through confession of the oneness,
Of the Creator of Creation.

# I Bind unto Myself Today

St. Patrick's Breastplate has been used as the basis for a lot of worship music. The best-known hymn setting was written in 1889 by an Irish-born Anglican woman named Cecil F. Alexander, the celebrated hymnist also responsible for "All Things Bright and Beautiful" and "Once in Royal David's City."

I bind unto myself today
the strong Name of the Trinity,
by invocation of the same,
the Three in One, and One in Three.

I bind this day to me forever,
by power of faith, Christ's Incarnation;
his baptism in Jordan river;
his death on cross for my salvation;
his bursting from the spicèd tomb;
his riding up the heavenly way;
his coming at the day of doom:
I bind unto myself today.

I bind unto myself today
the virtues of the starlit heaven,
the glorious sun's life-giving ray,
the whiteness of the moon at even,
the flashing of the lightning free,
the whirling wind's tempestuous shocks,

the stable earth, the deep salt sea,
around the old eternal rocks.

I bind unto myself today
the power of God to hold and lead,
his eye to watch, his might to stay,
his ear to hearken, to my need;
the wisdom of my God to teach,
his hand to guide, his shield to ward;
the word of God to give me speech,
his heavenly host to be my guard.

Christ be with me, Christ within me,
Christ behind me, Christ before me,
Christ beside me, Christ to win me,
Christ to comfort and restore me.
Christ beneath me, Christ above me,
Christ in quiet, Christ in danger,
Christ in hearts of all that love me,
Christ in mouth of friend and stranger.

I bind unto myself today
the strong Name of the Trinity,
by invocation of the same,
the Three in One, and One in Three.
Of whom all nature hath creation,
eternal Father, Spirit, Word:
praise to the Lord of my salvation,
salvation is of Christ the Lord.

# The Lorica of St. Patrick

The simplest form of the Lorica of St. Patrick is just the first lines of the longer, common version, invoking the protection of the Trinity.

I arise today
Through a mighty strength, the invocation of the Trinity,
Through the belief in the threeness,
Through confession of the oneness
Of the Creator of Creation.

# Nature

# NATURE

One of the distinctive qualities of Celtic spirituality is the presence of nature. Sometimes it is mingled with God as the Creator; sometimes it is the backdrop of daily life. But everywhere, nature is present and powerful.

# A Scottish Blessing

May the blessing of light be on you—
light without and light within.
May the blessed sunlight shine on you like a great peat
    fire,
so that stranger and friend may come and warm at it.
And may light shine out of the two eyes of you,
like a candle set in the window of a house,
bidding the wanderer come in out of the storm.

And may the blessing of the rain be on you,
may it beat upon your Spirit and wash it fair and clean,
and leave there a shining pool where the blue of Heaven
    shines,
and sometimes a star.

And may the blessing of the earth be on you,
soft under your feet as you pass along the roads,
soft under you as you lie out on it, tired at the end of day;
and may it rest easy over you when, at last, you lie out
    under it.
May it rest so lightly over you
that your soul may be out from under it quickly;
up and off and on its way to God.

# Song to the Sun

The eye of the great God,
The eye of the God of glory,
The eye of the King of Creation,
The eye of the Light of the living,
Pouring upon us
At each time and season,
Pouring upon us
Gently and generously.

Glory to you, Glorious sun.
Glory to you, sun,
Face of the God of life.

# New Moon

For the ancient Celts, this was a prayer said at the new moon while making the sign of the cross. It is popular today to use the first line of its second section when you encounter something in nature: "God who created you created me likewise."

> May your light be fair to me!
> May your course be smooth to me!
> If good to me is your beginning,
> Seven times better be your end,
> Fair moon of the seasons,
> Great lamp of grace!
>
> God who created you
> Created me likewise;
> God who gave you weight and light
> Gave to me life and death.

# The Beltane Blessing
## (Am Beannachadh Bealltain)

Beltane (Bealltain) is May Day, one of the four Celtic seasonal festivals. Beltane marks the beginning of the summer season when cattle, sheep, and goats are sent out to graze. A sheiling (or shieling), from the same root as shelter, is a seasonal or temporary hut used as a home by Scottish livestock farmers and their families while staying with their grazing animals during the summer. This blessing was used at the beginning of the season, looking forward to the year ahead and calling on the Trinity for protection and prosperity for the livestock and household.

Bless, O Threefold true and bountiful,
Myself, my spouse, and my children,
My tender children and their beloved mother at their head.
On the fragrant plain, on the gay mountain sheiling,
On the fragrant plain, on the gay mountain sheiling.

Everything within my dwelling or in my possession,
All cattle and crops, all flocks and corn,
From Hallow Eve to Beltane Eve,
With goodly progress and gentle blessing,
From sea to sea, and every river mouth,
From wave to wave, and base of waterfall.

Be the Three Persons taking possession of all to me
  belonging.
Be the sure Trinity protecting me in truth;
Oh! Satisfy my soul in the words of Paul,
And shield my loved ones beneath the wing of Your glory,
Shield my loved ones beneath the wing of Your glory.

Bless everything and everyone,
Of this little household by my side;
Place the cross of Christ on us with the power of love,
Till we see the land of joy,
Till we see the land of joy.

What time the cattle will forsake the stalls,
What time the sheep will forsake the folds,
What time the goats will ascend to the mount of mist,
May the tending of the Triune follow them,
May the tending of the Triune follow them.

Being who created me at the beginning,
Listen and attend me as I bend the knee to You,
Morning and evening as is becoming in me,
In Your own presence, O God of life,
In Your own presence, O God of life.

# Right It Is to Praise God

There is no plant in the ground
    But is full of God's virtue,
    There is no form in the strand
    But is full of God's blessing.
      Right it is to praise God.

There is no life in the sea,
    There is no creature in the river,
    There is nothing in the firmament,
    But proclaims God's goodness.
      Right it is to praise God.

There is no bird on the wing,
    There is no star in the sky,
    There is nothing beneath the sun,
    But proclaims God's goodness.
      Right it is to praise God.

# Prayers for
# the Start
# of the Day

# Toirt Taing (Giving Thanks)

Taing dhuit, a Dhé, gun d'éirich mi 'n diugh
Gu éirigh na beatha seo féin;
Gum b'ann gu d' ghlòir féin, a Dhé na fritheil,
Agus gu glòir m'anama d'a réir.

Dhé mhóir, dèan comhnadh air m'anam
Le comhnadh do thròcair féin;
Mar tha mis a' comhdach mo chuirp le olainn,
Comhdaich m'anam le faileas do sgéith.

Cuidich dhomh gach peacadh a sheachnadh,
Is ceann adhbhair gach peacaidh a thréig;
'S mar a sgaoileas an ceò air ceann nam beannaibh,
Gun sgaoileadh gach sgeòthaich bharr m'anam, a Dhé.

Thanks to you, O God, that I have risen today,
To the rising of this life itself;
May it be to Your own glory, O God of every gift,
And to the glory of my soul likewise.

O great God, aid You my soul
With the aiding of Your own mercy;
Even as I clothe my body with wool,
Cover You my soul with the shadow of Your wing.

Help me to avoid every sin,
And the source of every sin to forsake;
And as the mist scatters on the crest of the hills,
May each ill haze clear from my soul, O God.

# Bless to Me, O God

Bless to me, O God,
Each thing mine eye sees.

Bless to me, O God,
Each sound mine ear hears.

Bless to me, O God,
Each odor that goes to my nostrils.

Bless to me, O God,
Each taste that goes to my lips,
Each note that goes to my song,
Each ray that guides my way,
Each thing that I pursue,
Each lure that tempts my will.

The zeal that seeks my living soul,
The Three that seek my heart;
The zeal that seeks my living soul,
The Three that seek my heart.

# I Arise Today

From the ninth-century *Book of Cerne*

I arise today:
might of Heaven
brightness of Sun
whiteness of Snow
splendor of Fire
speed of Light
swiftness of Wind
depth of Sea
stability of Earth
firmness of Rock.

I arise today:
Might of God
Power of God
Wisdom of God
Eye of God
Ear of God
Word of God
Hand of God
Path of God
Shield of God
Host of God.

# God's Aid

This prayer has a message similar to that of St. Patrick's Breastplate— the common Celtic theme of God's immanent presence.

God to enfold me,
God to surround me,
God in my speaking,
God in my thinking.

God in my sleeping,
God in my waking,
God in my watching,
God in my hoping.

God in my life,
God in my lips,
God in my soul,
God in my heart.

God in my sufficing,
God in my slumber,
God in mine ever-living soul,
God in mine eternity.

# I Will Raise the Hearth-Fire

A prayer to be said first thing in the morning, originally while starting the fire..

I will raise the hearth-fire
   As Mary would.
   The encirclement of Bride and of Mary
   On the fire, and on the floor,
   And on the household all.

Who are they on the bare floor?
   John and Peter and Paul.
Who are they by my bed?
   The lovely Bride and her Fosterling.
Who are those watching over my sleep?
   The fair loving Mary and her Lamb.
Who is that anear me?
   The King of the sun it is.
Who is that at the back of my head?
   The Son of Life without beginning, without time.

# Prayers for
the End
of the Day

# The Aidan Compline

In monastic communities, compline, or night prayer, is offered at the end of the day before going to bed. Compline prayers look back on the day gone by, forward to the night's rest, and beyond to a new day. This prayer is attributed to Aidan, a member of the Celtic Christian monasteries Iona and Lindisfarne in the seventh century.

O Christ, Son of the living God,
may Your holy angels guard our sleep,
may they watch over us as we rest
and hover around our beds.

Let them reveal to us in our dreams
visions of Your glorious truth,
O High Prince of the universe,
O High Priest of the mysteries.

May no dreams disturb our rest
and no nightmares darken our dreams.
May no fears or worries delay
our willing, prompt repose.

May the virtue of our daily work
hallow our nightly prayers.
May our sleep be deep and soft
so our work be fresh and hard.

I will lie down and sleep in peace
for You alone, Lord, make me dwell in safety.
I will lie down and sleep in peace
for You alone, Lord, make me dwell in safety.

How precious to me are Your thoughts, O God!
How vast is the sum of them!
Were I to count them, they would outnumber the grains
of sand.
When I awake, I am still with You.

My Christ! My Christ!
My shield! My encircler!
Each day, each night,
each light, each dark.
Be near me, uphold me,
my treasure, my triumph.

Circle me, Lord,
keep protection near and danger afar.

Circle me, Lord,
keep light near and darkness afar.

Circle me, Lord,
keep peace within; keep evil out.

The peace of all peace be mine this night.

In the name of the Father, and of the Son, and of the
Holy Spirit. Amen.

# The Ita Compline

In the sixth century, Ita was an abbess in Limerick, Ireland. Her convent also ran a school for boys. A student of hers, Brendan, wrote this beloved compline prayer in the Celtic tradition and named it for her.

The Sacred Three
to save
to shield
to surround

the hearth
the home
this night
and every night.

Search me, O God, and know my heart.
Test me and know my thoughts.
See if there is any wicked way in me
and lead me in the way everlasting.

# Benediction for Rest

Bless to me, O God, the moon that is above me.
Bless to me, O God, the earth that is beneath me,
Bless to me, O God, my wife and my children,
And bless, O God, myself who have care of them;
Bless to me my wife and my children,
And bless, O God, myself who have care of them.

Bless, O God, the thing on which mine eye doth rest.
Bless, O God, the thing on which my hope doth rest,
Bless, O God, my reason and my purpose.
Bless, O bless Thou them. Thou God of life;
Bless, O God, my reason and my purpose,
Bless, O bless Thou them. Thou God of life.

Bless to me the bed-companion of my love.
Bless to me the handling of my hands.
Bless, O bless Thou to me, O God, the fencing of my
    defense.
And bless, O bless to me the angeling of my rest;
Bless, O bless Thou to me, O God, the fencing of my
    defense.
And bless, O bless to me the angeling of my rest.

# For Peace and Sleep

May the peace of the tallest mountain
and the peace of the smallest stone
be your peace.

May the stillness of the stars
watch over you.

May the everlasting
music of the wave
lull you to rest.

# O God of Life

O God of life, darken not to me Thy light,
O God of life, close not to me Thy joy,
O God of life, shut not to me Thy door,
O God of life, refuse not to me Thy mercy,
O God of life, quench Thou to me Thy wrath.
And O God of life, crown Thou to me Thy gladness,
O God of life, crown Thou to me Thy gladness.

# I Lie Down This Night

Like many Celtic Christian prayers, this brief nighttime prayer calls on the power and protection of the Trinity while we sleep.

I lie down this night with God,
And God will lie down with me.

I lie down this night with Christ,
And Christ will lie down with me.

I lie down this night with Spirit,
And the Spirit will lie down with me.

God and Christ and the Spirit
Be lying down with me.

# My Soul's Healer

My soul's Healer,
Keep me at even,
Keep me at morning,
Keep me at noon,
On rough course faring,
Help and safeguard
My means this night.
I am tired, astray, and stumbling,
Shield me from snare and sin.

# The Pilgrims' Safeguarding

Like the *loricas*, here is another example of a Celtic prayer seeking protection.

I am placing my soul and my body
Under your guarding this night, O Brigit,
O calm Fostermother of the Christ without sin,
O calm Fostermother of the Christ of wounds.

I am placing my soul and my body
Under your guarding this night, O Mary,
O tender Mother of the Christ of the poor,
O tender Mother of the Christ of tears.

I am placing my soul and my body
Under Your guarding this night, O Christ,
O Son of the tears, of the wounds, of the piercings,
May Your cross this night be shielding me.

I am placing my soul and my body
Under Your guarding this night, O God,
O Father of help to the poor feeble pilgrims,
Protector of earth and of heaven,
Protector of earth and of heaven.

# A Welsh Lullaby

Sleep, my babe, lie still and slumber,
All through the night.

Guardian angels God will lend thee,
All through the night.

Soft and drowsy hours are creeping,
Hill and vale in slumber sleeping,
Mother dear her watch is keeping,
All through the night.

God is here, you'll not be lonely,
All through the night.

'Tis not I who guards thee only,
All through the night.

Night's dark shades will soon be over,
Still my watchful care shall hover,
God with me His watch is keeping,
All through the night.

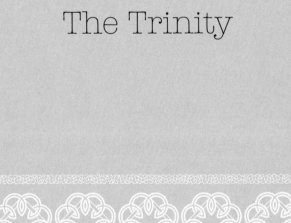

# The Trinity

# The Three

In name of Father,
In name of Son,
In name of Spirit,
Three in One:

Father cherish me,
Son cherish me,
Spirit cherish me,
Three all-kindly.

God make me holy,
Christ make me holy,
Spirit make me holy,
Three all-holy.

Three aid my hope,
Three aid my love,
Three aid mine eye,
And my knee from stumbling.

# The Compassing of God

The compassing of God and His right hand
Be upon my form and upon my frame;
The compassing of the High King and the grace of the
   Trinity
Be upon me abiding ever eternally,
Be upon me abiding ever eternally.

May the compassing of the Three shield me in my
   means,
The compassing of the Three shield me this day,
The compassing of the Three shield me this night
From hate, from harm, from act, from ill.
From hate, from harm, from act, from ill.

# Encompassing

The compassing of God be on you,
The compassing of the God of life.

The compassing of Christ be on you,
The compassing of the Christ of love.

The compassing of Spirit be on you,
The compassing of the Spirit of grace.

The compassing of the Three be on you,
The compassing of the Three preserve you,
The compassing of the Three preserve you.

# The Eye of God, the Foot of Christ, the Shower of the Spirit

Be the eye of God dwelling with you,
The foot of Christ in guidance with you,
The shower of the Spirit pouring on you,
Richly and generously,
God's peace be to you,
Jesus's peace be to you,
Spirit's peace be to you
And to your children.
Oh to you and to your children.

Each day and night
Of your portion in the world.
The compassing of the King of life be yours,
The compassing of loving Christ be yours,
The compassing of Holy Spirit be yours
Unto the crown of the life eternal,
Unto the crown of the life eternal.

The guarding of the God of life be on you,
The guarding of loving Christ be on you,
The guarding of Holy Spirit be on you
Every night of your lives,
To aid you and enfold you
Each day and night of your lives.

# The Sacred Three

The Sacred Three
My fortress be
Encircling me
Come and be
Round my heart and my home.

# Psalm 119

Psalm 119—the longest psalm in the Bible and, for that matter, the longest chapter, longer than many books in Scripture—holds a special place in the hearts of Celtic Christians. They feel an affinity to the Jews in the midst of their Exodus journey—both in being a historically nomadic people and in seeing the Exodus as a metaphor for life's spiritual journey. For early Celtic Christians, says Seán Ó Duinn, OSB, reciting Psalm 119 daily for a year symbolized the journey from Babylon to Jerusalem, from hell to heaven—into the presence of God.[2] Within Psalm 119 are several dozen prayers. Following are a few that would resonate especially with the Celtic Christians who chanted this psalm.

# The Servant's Prayer

Deal bountifully with your servant,
    so that I may live and observe your word.

Open my eyes, so that I may behold
    wondrous things out of your law.

I live as an alien in the land;
    do not hide your commandments from me.

My soul is consumed with longing
    for your ordinances at all times.

You rebuke the insolent, accursed ones,
    who wander from your commandments;

take away from me their scorn and contempt,
    for I have kept your decrees.

Even though princes sit plotting against me,
    your servant will meditate on your statutes.

Your decrees are my delight,
    they are my counselors.

—Psalm 119:17–24

# Prayer of Thanksgiving

Your word is a lamp to my feet
  and a light to my path.

I have sworn an oath and confirmed it,
  to observe your righteous ordinances.

I am severely afflicted;
  give me life, O LORD, according to your word.

Accept my offerings of praise, O LORD,
  and teach me your ordinances.

I hold my life in my hand continually,
  but I do not forget your law.

The wicked have laid a snare for me,
  but I do not stray from your precepts.

Your decrees are my heritage forever;
  they are the joy of my heart.

I incline my heart to perform your statutes
  forever, to the end.

—Psalm 119:105–112

# With My Whole Heart I Cry

With my whole heart I cry; answer me, O LORD.
　　I will keep your statutes.

I cry to you; save me,
　　that I may observe your decrees.

I rise before dawn and cry for help;
　　I put my hope in your words.

My eyes are awake before each watch of the night,
　　that I may meditate on your promise.

In your steadfast love hear my voice;
　　O LORD, in your justice preserve my life.

Those who persecute me with evil purpose draw near;
　　they are far from your law.

Yet you are near, O LORD,
　　and all your commandments are true.

Long ago I learned from your decrees
　　that you have established them forever.

—Psalm 119:145–152

# Wedding
# Blessings

# WEDDING BLESSINGS

The most common wedding blessing from the Celtic tradition may be "May the Road Rise Up to Meet You," but it was not originally meant for this purpose. Here are a few other blessings that were designed for weddings.

# Happy Is the Bride That Rain Falls On

This wedding blessing's opening line, by which it's known, is a wonderful example of the trickster playfulness and focus on nature that are so common in Celtic spirituality—being rained on is considered good luck.

Happy is the bride that rain falls on.
May your mornings bring joy and your evenings bring
   peace.
May your troubles grow few
as your blessings increase.

May the saddest day of your future
Be no worse than the happiest day of your past.
May your hands be forever clasped in friendship
And your hearts joined forever in love.

Your lives are very special,
God has touched you in many ways.
May his blessings rest upon you
And fill all your coming days.

We swear by peace and love to stand,
Heart to heart and hand to hand.
Hark, O Spirit, and hear us now,
Confirming this our Sacred Vow.

# A Child Every Year for You
# (Leanbh Gach Bliain Agat)

Sláinte agus saol agat
Bean ar do mhian agat
Leanbh gach bliain agat
Agus bás in Éirinn.

Health and life to you,
The woman of your choice for you,
A child every year for you,
And may you die in Ireland.

# May the Best You've Ever Seen

May the best you've ever seen
Be the worst you'll ever see.
May the mouse never leave your pantry
With a teardrop in his eye.
May you always keep healthy and hearty
Until you're old enough to die.
May you always be just as happy
As we wish you now to be.

# House
# Blessings

# A House Blessing

The peace of God,
The peace of men,
The peace of Columba kindly.
The peace of Mary mild, the loving,
The peace of Christ, King of tenderness,
The peace of Christ, King of tenderness.

Be upon each window,
Upon each door.
Upon each hole that lets in light.
Upon the four corners of my house,
Upon the four corners of my bed.
Upon the four corners of my bed.

Upon each thing my eye takes in,
Upon each thing my mouth takes in.
Upon my body that is of earth
And upon my soul that came from on high.
Upon my body that is of earth
And upon my soul that came from on high.

# God Bless the Corners
# of This House

This common Celtic house blessing might be found on a wall plaque in Ireland to this day.

God bless the corners of this house
And be the lintel blessed.
Bless the hearth, the table too
And bless each place of rest.

Bless each door that opens wide
To stranger, kith and kin;
Bless each shining window-pane
That lets the sunshine in.

Bless the roof-tree up above
Bless every solid wall.
The peace of Man, the peace of love,
The peace of God on all.

# Yule Chant

Prosperity be upon this dwelling,
   On all that you have heard and seen,
   On the bare bright floor flags,
   On the shapely standing stone staves,
   Hail King! Hail King! Blessed is He! Blessed is He!

Bless this house and all that it contains,
   From rafter and stone and beam;
   Deliver it to God from pall to cover,
   Be the healing of men therein,
   Hail King! Hail King! Blessed is He! Blessed is He!

Be in lasting possession of the house,
   Be you healthy about the hearth,
   Many be the ties and stakes in the homestead,
   People dwelling on this foundation,
   Hail King! Hail King! Blessed is He! Blessed is He!

Offer to the Being from found to cover,
   Include stave and stone and beam;
   Offer again both rods and cloth,
   Be health to the people therein,
   Hail King! Hail King! Blessed is He! Blessed is He!

# Other
# Blessings

May love and laughter light your days,
  and warm your heart and home.

May good and faithful friends be yours,
  wherever you may roam.

May peace and plenty bless your world
  with joy that long endures.

May all life's passing seasons
  bring the best to you and yours!

May the blessing of light be on you—
  light without and light within.

May the blessed sunlight shine on you
  and warm your heart
  till it glows like a great peat fire.

May you escape the gallows,
avoid distress,
and be as healthy as a trout.

Go raibh míle maith agat!
That you may have a thousand good things.

(Folks in Ireland still use this blessing in its original Gaelic as a general way of saying thank you.)

Go n-eirí an t-ádh leat.
That luck may rise with you.

Nár laga Dia thú.
May God never weaken you.

Rath Dé ort.
The grace of God on you.

Bail ó Dhia ort.
The blessing of God on you.

# Other
# Prayers

# The Journey Prayer

God, bless to me this day,
God, bless to me this night;
Bless, O bless.

God of grace,
Each day and hour of my life;
Bless, O bless.

God of grace,
Each day and hour of my life.
God, bless the pathway on which I go,
God, bless the earth that is beneath my sole.

Bless, O God, and give to me Your love,
O God of gods, bless my rest and my repose;
Bless, O God, and give to me Your love,
And bless, O God of gods, my repose.

# Here's to the Grey Goose

Mythical warrior Fionn mac Cumhaill (pronounced Finn McCool) unified tribal factions into a single Irish nation; his warriors were known as the Fianna. The collection of writings covering this epic saga is known as the Fenian Cycle. In the nineteenth and early twentieth centuries, the word *Fenian* referred to an Irish independence movement, and the word has become synonymous with Irish. This brief prayer hopes for Ireland to be a free nation with its own Irish king.

Here's to the grey goose
With the golden wing;
A free country
And a Fenian King.

# Bathing Prayer

*Crowdie* could refer to a mild cheese or a mix of raw oats and water. *Kail* is an old spelling of kale, and was also used simply to mean food. This delightful prayer is recorded in the *Carmina Gadelica* as one said with children while they're bathing, though the first verses seem to be a recipe for a creamy porridge.

A palmful for your age,
A palmful for your growth,
A palmful for your throat,
A flood for your appetite.

For your share of the dainty,
  Crowdie and kail;
For your share of the taking,
  Honey and warm milk.

For your share of the supping,
  Whisked whey and milk;
For your share of the spoil,
  With bow and with spear.

For your share of the preparation,
  The yellow eggs of Easter;
For your share of the treat,
  My treasure and my joy.

For your share of the feast,
  With gifts and with tribute;
For your share of the treasure,
  Pulset of my love.

For your share of the chase,
  Up the face of the Mountain of the Mist;
For your share of the hunting,
  And the ruling over hosts.

For your share of palaces,
  In the courts of kings;
For your share of Paradise,
  With its goodness and its peace.

The part of you that does not grow at dawn,
  May it grow at eventide;
The part of you that does not grow at night,
  May it grow at ridge of middle-day.

The three palmfuls of the Secret Three,
  To preserve you from every envy, evil eye, and death;
  The palmful of the God of Life,
  The palmful of the Christ of Love,
  The palmful of the Spirit of Peace,
  Triune of Grace.

# Grieve Not

Grieve not,
nor speak of me with tears.
But laugh and talk of me
as though I were beside you.
I loved you so,
'twas Heaven here with you.

# Bless to Me, O God

Bless to me, O God,
The path whereon I go;
Bless to me, O God,
The thing of my desire;
Evermore of evermore,
Bless to me my rest.

Bless to me the thing
Whereon is set my mind,
Bless to me the thing
Whereon is set my love;
Bless to me the thing
Whereon is set my hope;
O King of kings,
Bless to me mine eye!

# Notes

1   William Sharp, *The Dominion of Dreams: Under the Dark Star*, from the collection *The Writings of Fiona MacLeod* (New York: Duffield and Company, 1910), 423–24.

2   Calvin Miller, *Celtic Devotions* (Downers Grove, IL: IVP Books, 2008), 7–8.

# ABOUT PARACLETE PRESS

## WHO WE ARE

Paraclete Press is a publisher of books, recordings, and DVDs on Christian spirituality. Our publishing represents a full expression of Christian belief and practice—from Catholic to Evangelical, from Protestant to Orthodox.

We are the publishing arm of the Community of Jesus, an ecumenical monastic community in the Benedictine tradition. As such, we are uniquely positioned in the marketplace without connection to a large corporation and with informal relationships to many branches and denominations of faith.

## WHAT WE ARE DOING

PARACLETE PRESS BOOKS | Paraclete publishes books that show the richness and depth of what it means to be Christian. Although Benedictine spirituality is at the heart of all that we do, we publish books that reflect the Christian experience across many cultures, time periods, and houses of worship. We publish books that nourish the vibrant life of the church and its people.

We have several different series, including the best-selling Paraclete Essentials and Paraclete Giants series of classic texts in contemporary English; Voices from the Monastery—men and women monastics writing about living a spiritual life today; award-winning poetry; best-selling gift books for children on the occasions of baptism and first communion; and the Active Prayer Series that brings creativity and liveliness to any life of prayer.

MOUNT TABOR BOOKS | Paraclete's newest series, Mount Tabor Books, focuses on the arts and literature as well as liturgical worship and spirituality, and was created in conjunction with the Mount Tabor Ecumenical Centre for Art and Spirituality in Barga, Italy.

PARACLETE RECORDINGS | From Gregorian chant to contemporary American choral works, our recordings celebrate the best of sacred choral music composed through the centuries that create a space for heaven and earth to intersect. Paraclete Recordings is the record label representing the internationally acclaimed choir Gloriæ Dei Cantores, praised for their "rapt and fathomless spiritual intensity" by *American Record Guide*; the Gloriæ Dei Cantores Schola, specializing in the study and performance of Gregorian chant; and the other instrumental artists of the Arts Empowering Life Foundation.

Paraclete Press is also privileged to be the exclusive North American distributor of the recordings of the Monastic Choir of St. Peter's Abbey in Solesmes, France, long considered to be a leading authority on Gregorian chant.

PARACLETE VIDEO | Our DVDs offer spiritual help, healing, and biblical guidance for a broad range of life issues including grief and loss, marriage, forgiveness, facing death, bullying, addictions, Alzheimer's, and spiritual formation.

Learn more about us at our website:
www.paracletepress.com or phone us
toll-free at 1.800.451.5006

SCAN
TO
READ
MORE

*You may also be interested in . . .*

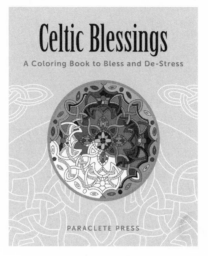

## Celtic Blessings
### A Coloring Book to Bless and De-Stress

ISBN: 978-1-61261-766-4, $11.99

Coloring these 30 Celtic patterns not only is a simple path to making something beautiful, but it has a spiritual element as well. Each design is paired with a traditional Irish blessing that will calm your spirit and quiet your mind.